Road Signs

by JoAnn Early Macken

amicus readers

1

Amicus Readers are published by Amicus
P.O. Box 1329, Mankato, Minnesota 56002

Printed in the United States of America at Corporate Graphics,
North Mankato, Minnesota.

Library of Congress Cataloging-in-Publication Data
Macken, JoAnn Early, 1953-
  Road signs / by JoAnn Early Macken.
    p. cm. -- (Amicus readers. My community)
  Includes index.
  Summary: "Describes common road signs you might see
around town and tells what they mean. Includes visual literacy
activity"--Provided by publisher.
  ISBN 978-1-60753-026-8 (library binding)
  1. Traffic signs and signals--Juvenile literature. I. Title.
  TE228.M2634 2011
  625.1'65--dc22
                    2010011109

Series Editor   Rebecca Glaser
Series Designer   Mary Herrmann
Book Designer   Darren Erickson
Photo Researcher   Heather Dreisbach

Photo Credits
Alan Eisen/iStockphoto, 11, 20 (one way); Anthony Berenyi/
Dreamstime.com, 9, 21 (speed limit); David Wilson/iStockpho-
to, 7, 21 (no parking); Gmeyerle/Dreamstime.com, 15; Image
Farm Inc., 5, 17, 20 (dead end); Shahrokh Rohani/iStockphoto,
cover, 1, 13, 20, 21 (curve); Terraxplorer/iStockphoto, 19

1223
42010

10 9 8 7 6 5 4 3 2 1

Contents

Road signs tell drivers what to do. Drivers must stop at stop signs. They look both ways. When it is clear, they can go.

A "P" stands for parking. A red circle with a slash means no. Cars cannot park here.

slash

7

Drivers must follow the law. A speed limit sign tells them how fast they can go. The number means miles per hour.

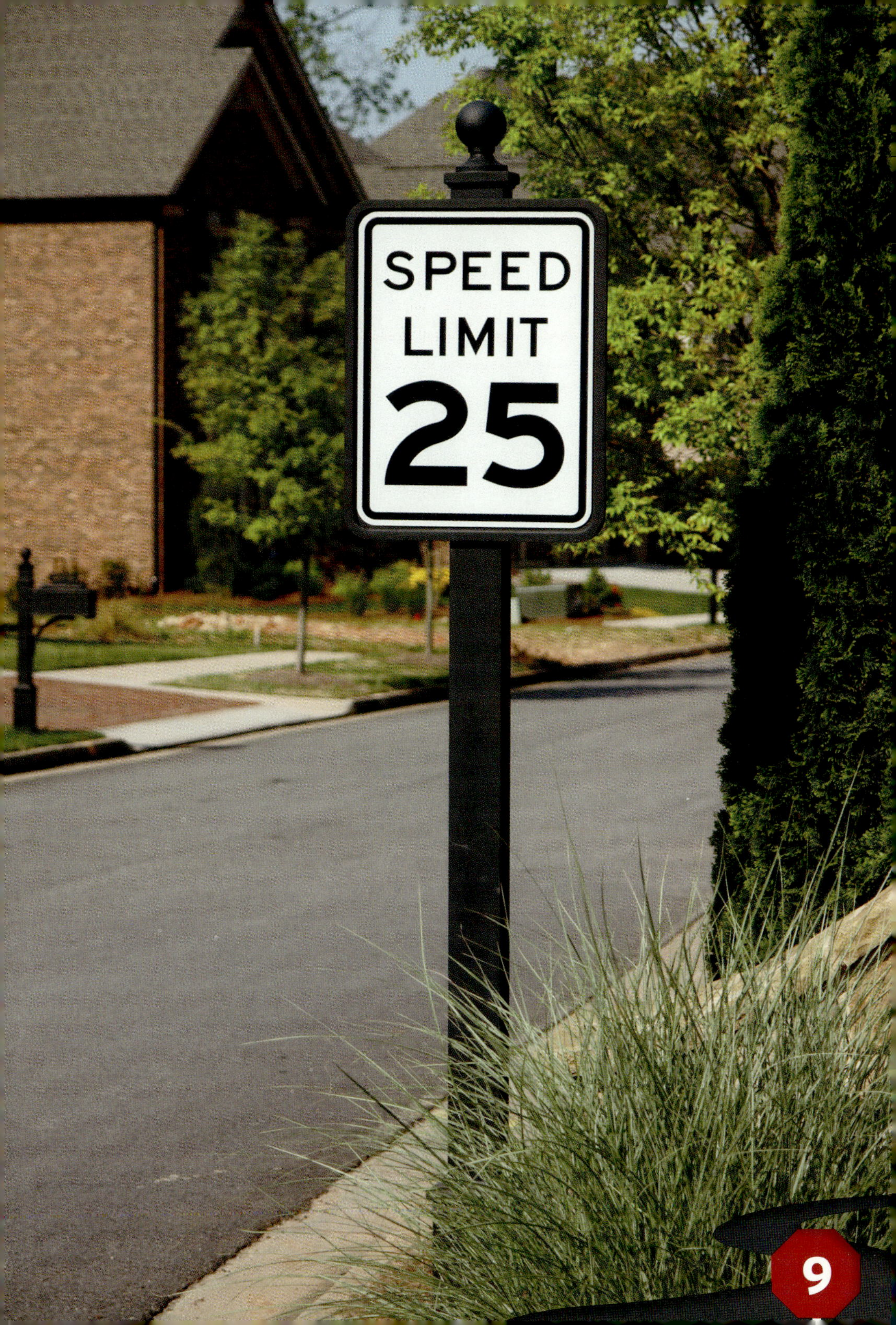
SPEED
LIMIT
25

On some roads, traffic moves only one way. An arrow shows drivers which way to go.

arrow

A warning sign is yellow. Its shape is a diamond. A curved arrow means that the road curves ahead.

curve

13

A railroad crossing sign looks like an X. Drivers must slow down, look, and listen. If a train is coming, they must wait.

RAILROAD CROSSING

2 TRACKS

A dead end is a street that has no way out. A sign tells drivers they cannot go through.

A sign with five sides means a school is nearby. Drivers must watch out for children. What signs do you see in your town?

19

Picture Glossary

arrow—a symbol that points one way

curve—a turn or bend

dead end—a street that has no way out

diamond—a shape with four sides that has its corners at the top, bottom, left, and right

slash—a slanted line

speed limit—the fastest speed that is safe and lawful. The number means miles per hour.

Road Signs: A Second Look

Take a second look at the photos in the book to answer these questions.

1. Which sign is red with white letters?

2. Which sign has people on it?

3. Which sign is shaped like a letter?

Check your answers on page 24.

Ideas for Parents and Teachers

My Community, an Amicus Readers Level 1 series, provides essential support for new readers while exploring children's first frame of reference, the community. Photo labels and a picture glossary help readers connect words and images. The activity page teaches visual literacy and critical thinking skills. Use the following strategies to engage your children or students.

Before Reading

- Ask the students if they have noticed any road signs when they have been riding around town with their family.
- Read the title and have the students talk about the cover photo. *Has anyone seen a sign like this? Does anyone know what it means?*

Read the Book

- Ask the students to read the book independently.
- Provide support where necessary. Show students how to use the photo labels and picture glossary if they need help with words.

After Reading

- Invite the students to return to the book and talk about the similarities and differences between the signs. Prompt them with questions, such as *How many signs have words on them? Which signs have arrows?*
- Have the students think about what might happen if drivers didn't obey road signs.

INDEX

WEB SITES

Road Signs Matching Game
http://www.lsuagcenter.com/en/4H/Kids/myworld/games/
Road+Signs+Matching+Game.htm

Traffic School for Kids
http://www.traffic-school-for-kids.com/traffic_school.htm

Traffic Sign Quiz for Kids
http://www.nysgtsc.state.ny.us/Kids/kidssign.htm

ANSWERS FROM PAGE 22

1. Stop sign

2. School crossing sign

3. Railroad crossing sign

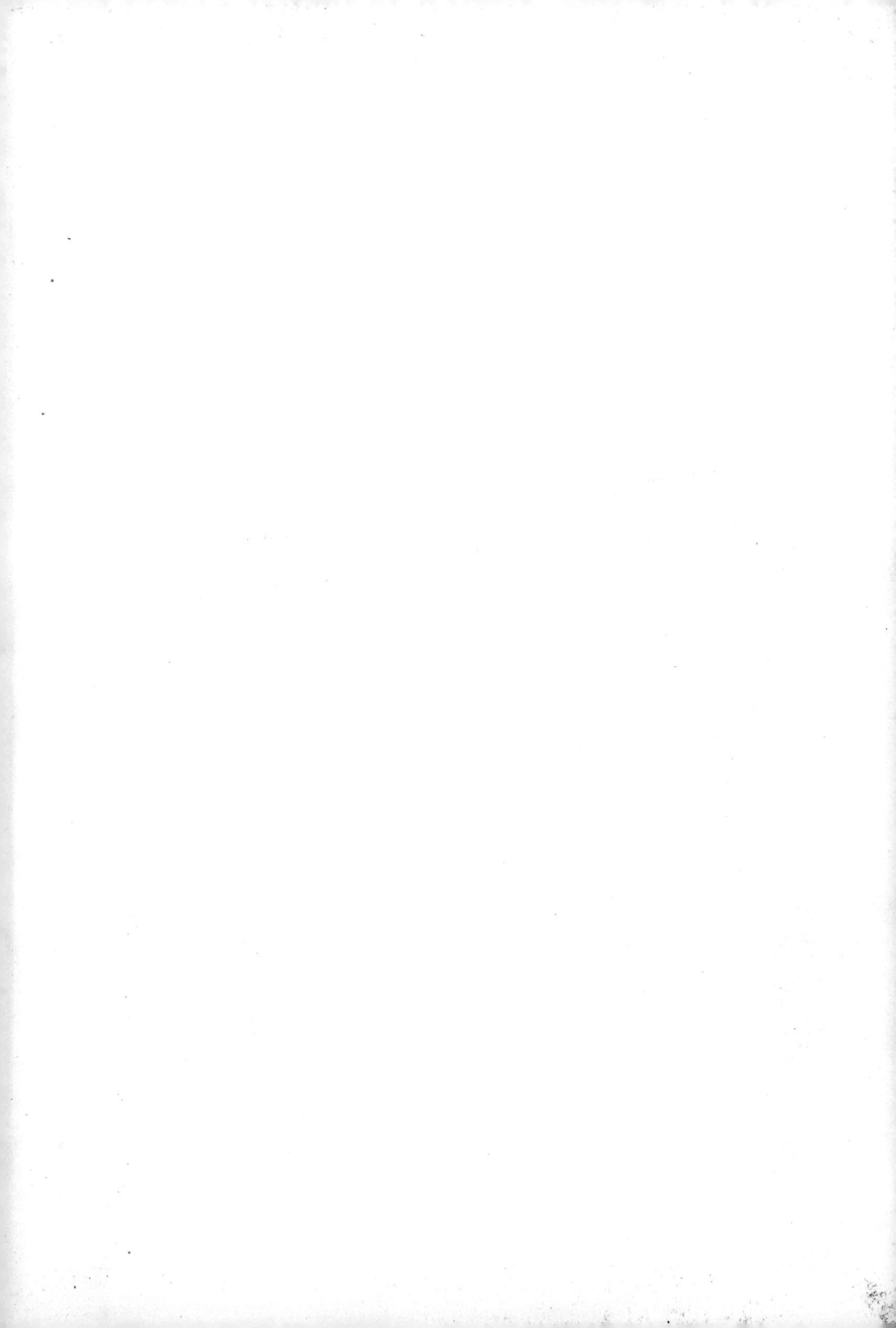